A Price That Matters

A Price That Matters

Britain's Disastrous
Exchange Rate Policy

John Mills

Civitas: Institute for the Study of Civil Society
London

First Published April 2012

© Civitas 2012
55 Tufton Street
London SW1P 3QL

email: books@civitas.org.uk

All rights reserved

ISBN 978-1-906837-37-2

Independence: Civitas: Institute for the Study of Civil Society is a registered educational charity (No. 1085494) and a company limited by guarantee (No. 04023541). Civitas is financed from a variety of private sources to avoid over-reliance on any single or small group of donors.

All publications are independently refereed. All the Institute's publications seek to further its objective of promoting the advancement of learning. The views expressed are those of the authors, not of the Institute.

Typeset by
Civitas

Printed in Great Britain by
Berforts Group Ltd
Stevenage SG1 2BH

Contents

	Page
Author	vi
Foreword David G. Green	vii
1. Britain's Disastrous Exchange Rate Policy	1
2. Origins of the Error	6
3. A More Competitive Exchange Rate	9
4. What Is To Be Done?	18
5. Doubts and Objections	23
Table 5.1: Exchange Rate Changes, Consumer Prices, the Real Wage, GDP, Industrial Output and Employment	26
6. Conclusion	35
Notes	39

Author

John Mills is an entrepreneur and economist. He graduated in Politics, Philosophy and Economics from Merton College, Oxford, in 1961. He is currently Chairman of John Mills Limited, a highly successful import-export and distribution company.

He has been Secretary of the Labour Euro-Safeguards Campaign since 1975 and the Labour Economic Policy Group since 1985. He has also been a Committee member of the Economic Research Council since 1997 and is now Vice-Chairman. He is also Chairman of The People's Pledge campaign for a referendum on Britain's EU membership.

He is the author of *Tackling Britain's False Economy* (Macmillan 1997), *Europe's Economic Dilemma* (Macmillan 1998), *Managing the World Economy* (Macmillan/Palgrave 2000), and *A Critical History of Economics* (Macmillan/Palgrave 2002).

Foreword

A wise government will try to adopt policies that encourage both full employment and an external balance of trade. Full employment suggests that as many people as possible are adding their bit to output, and an external balance implies mutually beneficial trade with other peoples. To achieve these aims careful co-ordination of monetary, fiscal and exchange-rate policies is required. However, in recent years governments have tended to disregard the exchange rate and to focus on inflation targeting, chiefly by manipulating the official interest rate.

John Mills argues that this lop-sided emphasis on inflation control has done great harm to our national prosperity. His work belongs in an emerging tradition of heterodox economic thought that draws on the best in Keynes and his rivals. Above all, this emerging approach contends that since the 1980s Britain has suffered from a kind of policy monoculture, focused too heavily on the inflation target. In the early 1980s, in the hope of squeezing out inflation, interest rates peaked at 17 per cent for a prolonged period and in the late 1980s and early 1990s they peaked at nearly 15 per cent. The resulting increases in the exchange rate made it impossible for many exporters to survive and sectors facing import competition suffered no less a decline. Our economy has still not recovered from the loss of manufacturing during that era.

For John Mills these were policy mistakes that are being continued to this day. The exchange rate is *A Price That Matters*.

David G. Green

1

Britain's Disastrous Exchange Rate Policy

The British economy is in dire shape. Growth is melting away. Unemployment is rising fast, with over one million young people between the ages of 16 and 24 out of work. Investment is wilting. Exports are flagging compared to imports. We have a very large and rising current account balance of payments deficit. The government is still spending much more than it raises in taxes and charges and no-one, not even the Chancellor of the Exchequer, now believes that this deficit is going to come anywhere near closing during the current parliament. As a result, government borrowing is rising fast, although the situation is actually much worse than is generally realised. Government liabilities are much higher than the usually quoted figures. If public sector pensions, financial interventions and Public Finance Initiative (PFI) commitments are all included, all the obligations on the government books already total about £2.5 trillion, or 167 per cent of GDP. Coping with all these liabilities, without unsustainable tax levels, depends on a much higher rate of economic growth than looks likely to have any chance of being achieved. Meanwhile mortgage debt stands at £1.2 trillion and unsecured consumer credit exceeds £210bn.[1] On top of all these other problems, the huge difficulties in the Eurozone and faltering political and economic policies in the USA make the prospects for the UK look even more uncertain.

As the outlook worsens and both government and private debt seem more and more difficult to get under control, fewer and fewer people believe that any of our politicians have policies which really are capable of coping adequately with our economic situation, however much our political leaders may say in public that they have a clear plan for the way ahead. Labour advocates reflation to bring down unemployment and to increase tax revenues, but any serious attempt to boost the economy in this way is bound to increase borrowing at least in the short term and to worsen the already dangerously high foreign payments deficit. This is all too likely to lead rapidly to the UK's credit rating being downgraded and interest costs rising. This does not, therefore, appear, at least on its own, to be a realistic policy. The Conscrvative-led Coalition is desperately trying to cut public expenditure to reduce the government deficit, but the rising costs of unemployment and all its associated costs, combined with falling tax revenues, have made the gap increasingly hard to close, as recent announcements clearly show.[2] In the meantime, the resurgence in private sector activity and employment that reduced public expenditure was supposed to achieve is nowhere in sight as both consumer and corporate confidence falter and the economy lurches towards a double-dip recession.

Is all this doom and gloom really inevitable? While there evidently are serious problems to be faced, is there really no practical alternative to our being resigned to years of privation and austerity? The message in this pamphlet is emphatic. We do not need to continue as we are. There is no reason at all, other than remediable policy errors, why we are in our present predicament. We are in the mess we are in not because we have to be but because we have chosen economic strategies which are deeply flawed. These economic strategies could easily have been different—and soon could be—if the right policy changes were made. Actually, it would be surprisingly easy to avoid all the austerity which now appears to be in prospect for the foreseeable future. This is because there is a compellingly simple and powerful explanation for the complex of problems that Britain—and most of the West—now faces. It has few awkward ideological overtones and dealing with it ought therefore to be acceptable to the vast majority of the population once they understand what is required. Unfortunately, however, what needs to be done is right off the spectrum of public discourse, as it has been for many years. It very urgently needs to get back into mainstream thinking because until we recognise what this elephant in the room is, we will never succeed in putting together policies which are going to get us out of our current bind.

The root problem is essentially simple and straightforward. Keeping inflation down to two per cent is not the most important policy goal, but getting the exchange rate and the cost base where it needs to be is absolutely crucial. Our fundamental problem is that the exchange rate policy which we have pursued for decades has made it much more expensive to run most manufacturing operations here than in other parts of the world, especially the countries round the Pacific Rim. As most foreign trade is in manufactured goods, we cannot pay our way in the world. This is why we have a chronic current account payments deficit—£46bn in 2010 alone[3]—which both sucks demand out of the economy and makes borrowing to fill the gap inevitable. It is the collapse of manufacturing caused by the UK's cost base being far too high which is at the root of our problems.

The cost base is so crucial because it is a measure of all the locally based costs which go into manufacturing. Typically, of all cost inputs, about 20 per cent is raw materials and ten per cent covers depreciation of fixed assets such as plant and machinery. For all of these cost factors there are world prices which governments in any individual country can do little to influence. Of the remaining 70 per cent—leaving aside a target profit ratio of, say, ten per cent—about 60 per cent consists of local costs, of which the vast majority are ultimately for wages and salaries. The rate at which these locally based costs are charged out to the rest of the world is set by the exchange rate and this is a factor over which any government can have a large amount of influence, if it is determined to exercise it. If the exchange rate, and hence the cost base, is too high, manufacturing will migrate elsewhere. If it is low, manufacturing will be strongly attracted.

It is sometimes argued that the exchange rate does not matter because countries with high parities can always move up-market and make more and more sophisticated products, and thus stay competitive. It is indeed true that Britain has managed to compete successfully in a number of key industries such as pharmaceuticals, motor vehicles, arms and aircraft engines. Just because some industries remain competitive, however, does not alter the fact that many others—particularly those less protected by intellectual property rights or producing simpler products—find it far harder to compete in high cost base conditions and frequently go to the wall. Furthermore countries with strong manufacturing bases also move up market and then become threats to the industrial survivors in countries like the UK. In the end it is the average which counts and measured in this way British industry is unfortunately heavily handicapped. This is why we have for many years had a huge visible trade deficit—about £95bn in 2010, or 6.5 per cent of our National Income.[4]

The bottom line is that the UK has allowed the cost base to be far too high for far too long. This is why our manufacturing base has been eroded and why our living standards, which were the highest in the world in the nineteenth century, are now lower than those in about 20 other countries.[5] There is no solution to our current economic problems unless we can get our cost base down. And this is almost entirely an exchange rate issue on which governments can have a decisive impact if they are minded to do so.

2

Origins of the Error

How did this situation come about? Again, there is a simple answer. Much of the explanation lies in a big change in intellectual fashion. When, during the 1970s, inflation increased rapidly across the whole of the western world, fuelled by monetary excesses following the dollar devaluation in 1971 and enormous—although in real terms temporary—increases in commodity costs, particularly oil, Keynesianism fell out of fashion and monetarism took its place. When price rises took off, therefore—rising in the UK by 24 per cent between 1974 and 1975—almost everyone agreed that getting inflation down was the top economic policy priority and that restricting the money supply was the way to do it. As a result, all the available weapons were brought into play. Interest rates were raised dramatically so that, for example, for the whole of the 1980s, UK Treasury Bill rates averaged over ten per cent.[1] The money supply was tightened. Credit was restricted. Unemployment rose—and inflation fell back. Unfortunately, almost no-one was concerned with what all these policies did to the exchange rates both in the UK and elsewhere in the western economies compared to the Pacific Rim countries. In fact, hardly surprisingly, they shot up, especially in real terms after allowing for very high levels of inflation. In the UK, by 1982 the pound had gone up in value by a mind boggling 64 per cent against all other currencies compared to its value in 1977.[2] This happened, moreover, just as China, which was barely at the time on any western economic policy maker's radar screen, was just moving into the trading world. At the same time, the Tiger economies—South Korea, Hong Kong, Taiwan and Singapore—were getting fully into their strides as major world trading economies. The West, which in most cases already had cost bases which were not very competitive compared to other parts of the world, suddenly had them jacked up as a result of the implementation of monetarist policies to combat inflation so that they became far higher than they were in the East, and this is how it has stayed ever since. As a direct and ineluctable consequence, a huge amount of manufacturing activity left the West and moved to the East. We deindustrialised and they reaped all the benefit.

Forty years later, keeping inflation down is still the top economic priority. The Bank of England's target is two per cent. The European Central Bank's is even lower. The US Fed's is about the same. The theory is that low inflation keeps interest rates down and will lead to economic growth, but this is not what has happened. Growth rates in the West are far below those in the East and have been for many decades now. By far the biggest reason why this has happened is that the real exchange rates between West and East which were established in the 1970s have never changed significantly since then bar some fluctuation. Concentrating on inflation and ignoring the exchange rate has been a catastrophic policy error for the UK and for all the western countries which have allowed this to happen.

3

A More Competitive Exchange Rate

Britain has not had a sufficiently competitive exchange rate to attract manufacturing on a major scale compared to the rest of the world since the nineteenth century. Our economy grew by a remarkable amount in the 1930s after the 24 per cent devaluation in 1931,[1] when Britain came off the Gold Standard and for a brief period we had a competitive pound. In the five years between 1932 and 1937, manufacturing output rose 48 per cent to 38 per cent above the 1929 peak.[2] Unemployment fell sharply as the number of people with jobs quickly increased. Over the period between 1931 and 1937, the number of those in work rose from 18.7m to 21.4m as 2.7m new jobs were created, half of them in manufacturing.[3] This shows how critically important the cost base, very largely determined by the exchange rate, really is. The British economy grew faster in the five years between 1932 and 1937—at a cumulative 4.6 per cent per annum —than for any other five-year period in our history, showing clearly how effective a radical expansionist policy could be, against the most unpromising background of the time.

Getting the exchange rate right, therefore, makes a huge difference, setting the scene for making all the other complementary policies needed to run a successful economy work well. Any country with a low exchange rate—such as China—will have four massive advantages over any country—like the UK—with a high one. These are:

1. The competitive economy's manufacturing base will grow more rapidly than the world average and its share of world trade will rise.

2. It is much easier to achieve productivity gains in manufacturing than in most of the service sector, so that any economy with exceptionally competitive exports will grow more rapidly than the world average.

3. Highly competitive economies benefit from a better spread of employment opportunities both geographically and in socio-economic terms than if they depend very heavily on services.

4. Countries with highly competitive exports are very unlikely to find their economic policies constrained by balance of payments problems.

World trade consists partly of commodities, partly services, but by far the largest component—about 60 per cent for most modern diversified economies—is manufactured goods. If any country—like the UK—has a weak manufacturing base, it will therefore tend to have problems paying its way in the world—and indeed we do. Deficits then have to be financed either by selling assets or by borrowing. Any current account deficit has, therefore, to be matched pound for pound by an exactly equivalent amount of capital receipts. These can take the form of either selling assets such as shares in UK companies, or direct investment or borrowing, in exactly the same way as any individual who spends more than his income has to draw on capital or borrow to make up the difference.

There is another crucial problem about a foreign payments deficit. If what we sell to the world is less than we buy, purchasing power gets sucked out of the economy—a total of £46bn in the UK in 2010 after taking all international transactions into account. There are three ways in which this can be counteracted, to avoid this gap in demand depressing the economy. Either, consumers have to spend more than their incomes or the government has to spend more than its revenues or businesses have to invest more than they save. At the moment investment in the corporate sectors is low and its cash savings are high, so all the gap and more has to be filled by consumer and government borrowing. There is thus a direct causal link between the exchange rate and borrowing. If the exchange rate is too high, it leads to a current account foreign payments deficit. The only way then to maintain demand in the economy is by consumer and government debt increasing.

Does this matter? Yes, indeed it does, especially if, to keep plugging the deficits in the country's, the consumers' and the government's expenditure, more and more debt has to be created in relation to the borrowers' capacity to repay. This is exactly what has happened to us. Provided lenders are satisfied that, in the last analysis, the debts owing to them will be honoured and in the meantime interest on them will be paid, borrowing can carry on going up and up—as it does, for example, to growing and profitable companies. Unfortunately, however, neither countries with weak payment balances, nor their consumers, nor their governments, generate the sorts of income flows which are produced by profitable corporate investments. Very significant constraints on borrowing then come into play.

When the sums owed both by consumers and the government begin to look uncomfortably large, lenders get increasingly unsure about lending to them. They also start to worry about the country's capacity to meet its obligations. To stop the country's current account payments deficit getting too substantial, the economy therefore cannot be run at full stretch because this would widen the payments gap to an unsustainable extent. A weak balance of payments position thus makes it impossible to run the economy at full throttle. The cumulative effect of this constraint explains why unemployment, running at about 2.6m in the UK during the autumn of 2011, is so high. Actually, the headline unemployment figure, bad as it is, grossly underestimates the real total number of people who would be willing to work if there were sufficient jobs available that paid a reasonable wage. Surveys, including a recent one compiled by the TUC, show that the total number of missing jobs is nearer 4.9m than 2.6m.[4]

As deflationary polices bite harder and growth stalls, constraints tighten still further. If any economy has a large borrowing requirement which is rising more slowly than the economy is growing—like India does at the moment—lenders can remain reasonably confident that their debts will be repaid. If the debts are rising faster than the growth rate—which is now the position in the UK and much of the rest of the West, and particularly in much of the Eurozone—as soon as it becomes apparent that this is the case, lenders start getting much more nervous. Their reaction then is both to raise interest rates to compensate for the increased lending risk and to try to reduce their exposure to the debt. But these can very easily turn into self-defeating policies. The less borrowing there is to make up the demand deficiency, the more slowly the economy will grow and the less debt-servicing capacity the economy will have. Meanwhile the need for borrowing may not go down. If consumers' incomes drop more rapidly than their spending and claims on government expenditure rise faster than before as unemployment goes up, the need for more debt may go up rather than down. Indeed, as long as there is a current account balance of payments deficit, this is bound to happen.

This is the bind in which the UK government now finds itself. With the exchange rate and the cost base where they are at the moment, no mix of policies which is on the horizon will work. Neither Labour reflation nor Conservative/Lib Dem cuts are viable. If we carry on the way we are at the moment, at best we will suffer from years of slow or quite possibly negative growth, rising unemployment, stagnant or falling real incomes, and cutbacks in government expenditure. At worst, our capacity to go on borrowing the money we need to plug the unending deficits with which we will be confronted will lead to lenders losing patience with us. Our ability to borrow more money on any viable terms will then disappear. A really major crisis will be precipitated. We will drift into the same predicament as hopelessly uncompetitive Eurozone economies such as Greece and Portugal now face.

The root problem, which we in most of the West now face, can therefore be simply stated. We have been chasing the wrong economic goal and we have been doing so for a long time. Keeping inflation down to two per cent, the Bank of England's target, or even less in the case of the European Central Bank, with the Fed's goal being about the same, is not the most significant objective. Getting the exchange rate at the right level is far more important. The theory that low inflation keeps interest rates down and will therefore lead to economic growth has not worked in practice and it never will. The problem is that all the policy instruments needed to keep inflation at very low levels are exactly those which keep the exchange rate and the cost base up. This is why the West has deindustrialised, and this in turn is why we have such problems with our balance of payments and hence, unemployment, low or non-existent growth and both government and sovereign deficits, leading to more and more borrowing. Furthermore, because growth rates in the West are far below those in the East, we are steadily losing influence, self-confidence and ability to deal with world problems from a basis of solvency and self-assurance. We are rapidly heading downhill and all because of nothing which is inevitable. Just bad policies which we should never have adopted but which luckily are not impossible to reverse, once the will to do so is there.

What, then, do we need to do to unwind the mistakes which have dogged British economic history for far too long but right now in an even more acute form than at any time since the 1970s and 80s? The answer is essentially fairly simple. We need to cease trying to fight inflation as our major objective. Instead, we need to get the exchange rate and the cost base right, so that we can attract back enough manufacturing and services—but mainly manufacturing—to enable us to pay our way in the world. If we can do this, we can get rid of our weak balance of payments position which, in turn, is the only long-term way to stop the country, its consumers and its government needing to borrow more and more money with less and less chance of being able to pay it back. It will enable us to have a much more prosperous future. In addition, it will avoid our position in the world sliding downhill as a result of our inability to run our economy effectively. It will then strengthen our capacity to help solve some of the world's longer term problems from a position of solvency and confidence rather than weakness and decline.

What would we have to do with the exchange rate to get our economy functioning much better? Some fairly easy calculations provide the order of magnitude of the devaluations which would need to be made to deal with various different objectives. They start from where we are now with £1.00 = about $1.60 and around €1.15 and assume, for the moment, that we devalue and—at least for the time being—no other countries do so too. The results are as follows:

1. To eliminate the payments deficit, leaving the economy capable of growing at about two per cent per annum but still with large levels of unemployment, a devaluation of between ten per cent and 15 per cent would be needed.

2. To eliminate the payments deficit and to provide enough leeway to allow the economy to be run with a much higher level of demand, producing a cumulative growth rate of about four per cent per annum—about the world average—a devaluation of between 20 per cent to 25 per cent would be required.

3. To enable the UK economy to move over a transitional period to the growth rates experienced by countries such as Germany and Japan after World War II, or China now—i.e. with a growth rate of about eight per cent per annum—the pound would need to fall in value on the exchanges by 40 per cent to 50 per cent.

It is important to realise that these parity changes need to be on a trade weighted basis to be effective. This means that we need to allow for the impact of other countries in the West following our example and reducing their exchange rates at the same time as the UK. Obviously, to the extent that this happens, the increase in the UK's competitiveness will be reduced. If other countries were to devalue at the same time as the UK then even larger devaluations against the non-devaluing countries would be required. The magnitude of the changes needed even before taking this factor into account is, however, an important testament to the enormous lack of competitiveness, particularly with many of the Pacific Rim countries, to which Britain is currently exposed.

How likely is it that we would be faced with other countries devaluing with us, thus diluting the impact of the pound coming down? At the moment, the prospects for other countries following suit do not look that large. As long as the Eurozone holds together, Germany's huge export surplus is likely to keep the international value of the euro up. If the Eurozone breaks up, our main trading partners in the EU, particularly Germany, would be certain to see their currencies rapidly revaluing, which would be the mirror of what needs to be done in the UK. Since the dollar is still the world's major reserve currency, a major US devaluation matching ours is not that probable. It is also unlikely that the rest of the world would pay much attention to what we do with our currency because we are not now major players in world trading terms. When sterling fell by about 20 per cent between 2006 and 2008 from its previous stratospheric level, there were few international repercussions. Why should there be any more if the pound fell to, say, $1.20 and €0.85?

4

What Is To Be Done?

What would need to be done to get the exchange rate down? There would have to be a major reversal of the policy objectives which policy-makers in the UK have long strived to attain. The authorities would need to make it clear that a much lower pound was not only what they wanted to see, but what they were determined to achieve. The Bank of England would have to be instructed to sell sterling and buy foreign currencies. More quantitative easing should be introduced, supplemented by lending directly by the Bank of England to organisations capable of paying the money back from income flows, such as local authorities and housing associations. This would enable them to finance house building. The government should deliberately increase its spending in relation to its revenues to widen the foreign payments deficit temporarily, to assist in making the parity of the currency fall.

The nationalised banks would need to be instructed to lend more money to businesses, accepting the risk that there might be more bad loans. Inward investment—allowing the shares in UK companies, such as Cadbury's to be sold to foreign buyers—should be discouraged instead of being welcomed, as it has been, because, apart from any other considerations, the huge capital infusions to sterling from these kinds of transactions drive up the exchange rate. If the credit rating agencies threaten downgrades, they should be ignored—even encouraged—because negative postings from them would help to bring the pound down. If interest rate rises are threatened, they should be counteracted by the Bank of England simply printing more money, instead of it having to be borrowed from the markets.

All of this is technically feasible but there would be potentially three major obstacles in the way. One would be the attitude of the countries against whom we were devaluing. The second would be concerns about whether it would in practice be possible to get the pound down. The third would be entrenched views on economic policy within the UK and most other western countries about the relevance of the exchange rate in relation to other much more conventional economic policy objectives.

Countries, such as China in the east, and others elsewhere, may well object to losing some of their competitiveness with us but, on mature reflection, they may realise that they have little to lose and much to gain from countries such as the UK being in better financial and economic shape. It is not in anyone's interest for there to be a massive debt crisis in the West, undermining the prosperity of the world economy generally and the prospects for everyone's exports in particular. Nor is it in the long-term interest of countries such as China to run its present large balance of payments surplus, especially if the foreign exchange thus generated is lent to countries which are never likely to be able to pay it back.

China's very rapid growth rate would only be impacted if the UK and other western countries adopted very deep devaluations, which would be much more difficult to achieve than smaller ones. For depreciations of anything up to about 25 per cent against the Chinese Renminbi, there would not be much erosion, if any, to China's huge manufacturing capacity.

It might be argued on more general grounds that it would be unfair for Britain to bring the value of the pound down because other countries, especially those in the West, would be adversely affected. There is, however, no reason why they should be. If our export prices were lower and our output more competitive, all the countries to which we export would benefit from better value for money on the goods they buy from us. When we could be severely criticised would be if we were to run a balance of payments surplus, which would have to be matched by extra deficits elsewhere, but it would make no sense for us to allow this to happen. In fact the real international culprits are countries such as China, Germany, Switzerland, Taiwan and Japan which have consistently run balance of payments surpluses year after year, thus forcing deficit countries into penury. We should not do this and there is no reason why we should contemplate doing so. Provided we do not go down this road, there is no reason why it would be unreasonable for us to have enough manufacturing and export generating capacity to pay our way in the world. We very urgently need to get to this position and if no international consensus was forthcoming there would still be nothing to stop the UK taking the unilateral actions described above. It would clearly be better to achieve some measure of acceptance of the reasons why we needed to do what had to be done, but in the last analysis, this would not be essential.

Would it, however, actually be possible to get the value of the pound down by perhaps 25 per cent from where it is now, even assuming that all the policies for doing so outlined above were put into effect? There is certainly plenty evidence from our recent economic history that allowing the pound to become too strong is feasible. Few people now deny that this was the position particularly in the early 1980s as monetarism drove up the exchange rate to completely unsustainable levels, or during the ERM period running up to 1992, or during the 2000s as the parity of the pound rose to $2.00. The issue is whether, if the policies which caused these over-valuations were reversed, they would get the pound down as successfully as doing everything possible to keep the pound up kept it too strong during the periods of acute over-valuation.

Clearly, controlling the exchange rate is more difficult with a floating currency than when exchange rates are fixed, especially against the background of the huge sums being traded across the exchanges every day. Historical evidence, however, indicates that devaluations can be achieved if the governments concerned are determined enough to make sure they happen. The impact of the Plaza Accord in 1985 achieved a huge weakening of the US dollar, with its value falling against all other currencies by almost 45 per cent between 1984 and 1987.[1] Our own recent experience as the value of sterling fell from $2.00 in 2007 to about $1.60 in 2009 is surely also instructive. So are all the many other devaluations which have been achieved, some of which are highlighted in table 5.1 (pp. 26-30). If, moreover, it turned out to be impossible to get the pound down without exchange controls on capital movements—which seems to be extremely unlikely—at the very worst we might be left with a choice of some constraints on foreign exchange movements, or endless deflation. Would it really be sensible in these improbable circumstances necessarily to rule out all constraints on capital movements if the alternative was unending austerity?

5

Doubts and Objections

The biggest objections, well founded or not, are likely to come from everyone in the UK who is inured to different policy objectives. Politicians and civil servants, who have fought for low inflation and ignored the significance of the exchange rate for decades, supported by almost all the media and academia, are unlikely to change their minds quickly. Importers are bound to oppose devaluation and so will all those who regard cheap foreign holidays as a prize not to be foregone. The City has always tended to favour a strong pound because of the increased leverage this provides everyone involved in international transactions. Pensioners and others fear that the accommodating monetary policy and low interest rates which go with low exchange rates may adversely affect them, which may well be true in the short term. In the longer term, however, good pensions are only affordable if the economy can be made to grow to pay for them. There are also four other arguments against devaluation which undoubtedly would carry weight with those who would be inclined to oppose a change in policy along the lines proposed in this pamphlet, and these need to be dealt with in some detail.

A fall in living standards?

First, it is frequently argued that devaluations lower living standards. If lowering the exchange rate makes the economy grow more quickly than it otherwise would have done—which always happens—this argument cannot, however, be correct. In the end, living standards are determined by the national income divided by the number of people in the country. If the national income goes up but the number of inhabitants stays the same, national income per head must increase. It is true that there will inevitably be some losers as well as many winners, but on average everyone must be better off, particularly in the longer term. It is also true that if the percentage of national income devoted to investment goes up, the proportion going to consumption must go down, and this has to be reflected in more savings. As incomes rise, therefore, the savings ratio will have to increase—which urgently needs to happen for other familiar reasons. This will not affect average total incomes, however, only the proportion of income which is saved rather than consumed. On average, everyone will be better off in the short term and much better off in the medium and long term.

This is exactly what happened in Britain not only in the 1930s but much more recently when we came out of the Exchange Rate Mechanism (ERM) in 1992. Wages rose faster than the Consumer Price Index (CPI) and everyone in employment, on average, became better off. Everyone in Britain continued to spend in sterling as well as getting paid in pounds, so that they were insulated from the fact that, measured against international currencies, the pound was a good deal cheaper. This, however, made a big difference to the competitiveness of British exports, which in turn drove a significant increase in British industrial output. Output rose by 2.2 per cent in 1993 and 5.4 per cent in 1994, having fallen by 3.3 per cent in 1991, the last full year when we were in the ERM.

Nor is what happened to Britain in the 1930s and the 1990s exceptional. The pattern has been repeated time after time when any of the many major devaluations and revaluations which have taken place in recent years are considered. The table below shows what has happened, including cases such as Argentina and Iceland. Their devaluations have been much greater than anything proposed in this pamphlet. Even major depreciations like these, however, caused by crises which caused large-scale temporary disruption, are followed within a year or two by rapid recovery. More gentle devaluations, on the scale that this pamphlet recommends, generally show no significant—if any—reductions in living standards as wages rise faster than the cost of living.

Table 5.1 Exchange Rate Changes, Consumer Prices,
the Real Wage, GDP, Industrial Output and Employment

All figures are year on year percentage changes except for unemployment

	Year	Con-sumer Prices	Wage Rates	Real Wage Change	GDP Change	Industrial Output Change	Unem-ployment Per Cent
Britain - 31% Devaluation against the dollar and 24% against all currencies in 1931	1930	-6.0	-0.7	5.3	-0.7	-1.4	11.2
	1931	-5.7	-2.1	3.6	-5.1	-3.6	15.1
	1932	-3.3	-1.7	1.6	0.8	0.3	15.6
	1933	0.0	-0.1	-0.1	2.9	4.0	14.1
	1934	0.0	1.5	1.5	6.6	5.5	11.9
France - 27% Devaluation against all currencies in 1957/58	1956	2.0	9.7	7.7	5.1	9.4	1.1
	1957	3.5	8.2	4.7	6.0	8.3	0.8
	1958	15.1	12.3	-2.8	2.5	4.5	0.9
	1959	6.2	6.8	0.6	2.9	3.3	1.3
	1960	3.5	6.3	2.8	7.0	10.1	1.2
	1961	3.3	9.6	6.3	5.5	4.8	1.1

	Year	Con-sumer Prices	Wage Rates	Real Wage Change	GDP Change	Industrial Output Change	Unem-ployment Per Cent
USA - 28% Devaluation against all currencies over 1985/87	1984	4.3	4.0	-0.3	6.2	11.3	7.4
	1985	3.6	3.9	0.3	3.2	2.0	7.1
	1986	1.9	2.0	0.1	2.9	1.0	6.9
	1987	3.7	1.8	-1.9	3.1	3.7	6.1
	1988	4.0	2.8	-1.2	3.9	5.3	5.4
	1989	5.0	2.9	-2.1	2.5	2.6	5.2
Japan - 47% Revaluation against all currencies over 1990/94	1989	2.3	3.1	0.8	4.8	5.8	2.3
	1990	3.1	3.8	0.7	4.8	4.1	2.1
	1991	3.3	3.4	0.1	4.3	1.8	2.1
	1992	1.7	2.1	0.4	1.4	-6.1	2.2
	1993	1.3	2.1	0.8	0.1	-4.6	2.5
	1994	0.7	2.3	1.6	0.6	0.7	2.9

	Year	Consumer Prices	Wage Rates	Real Wage Change	GDP Change	Industrial Output Change	Unemployment Per Cent
Italy - 20% Devaluation against all currencies over 1990/93	1990	6.4	7.3	0.9	2.1	-0.6	9.1
	1991	6.3	9.8	3.5	1.3	-2.2	8.6
	1992	5.2	5.4	0.2	0.9	-0.6	9.0
	1993	4.5	3.8	-0.7	-1.2	-2.9	10.3
	1994	4.0	3.5	-0.5	2.2	5.6	11.4
	1995	5.4	3.1	-2.3	2.9	5.4	11.9
Finland - 24% Devaluation against all currencies over 1991/93	1990	6.1	9.4	3.3	0.0	-0.1	3.5
	1991	4.1	6.4	2.3	-7.1	-9.7	7.6
	1992	2.6	3.8	1.2	-3.6	2.2	13.0
	1993	2.1	3.7	1.6	-1.6	5.5	17.5
	1994	1.1	7.4	6.3	4.5	10.5	17.4
	1995	1.0	4.7	3.7	5.1	7.8	16.2

	Year	Consumer Prices	Wage Rates	Real Wage Change	GDP Change	Industrial Output Change	Unemployment Per Cent
Spain – 18% Devaluation against all currencies over 1992/94	1991	5.9	8.2	2.3	2.3	-0.7	16.3
	1992	5.9	7.7	1.8	0.7	-3.2	18.5
	1993	4.6	6.8	2.2	-1.2	-4.4	22.8
	1994	4.7	4.5	-0.2	2.1	7.5	24.1
	1995	4.7	4.8	0.1	2.8	4.7	22.9
	1996	3.6	4.8	1.2	2.2	-0.7	22.2
Britain – 19% Devaluation against all currencies in 1992	1990	9.5	9.7	0.2	0.6	-0.4	6.8
	1991	5.9	7.8	1.9	-1.5	-3.3	8.4
	1992	3.7	11.3	7.6	0.1	0.3	9.7
	1993	1.6	3.2	1.6	2.3	2.2	10.3
	1994	2.4	3.6	1.2	4.4	5.4	9.6
	1995	3.5	3.1	-0.4	2.8	1.7	8.6

	Year	Consumer Prices	Wage Rates	Real Wage Change	GDP Change	Industrial Output Change	Unemployment Per Cent
Argentina – 72% Devaluation against all currencies early 2002	2000	-1.1	1.2	3.3	-0.8	-0.3	14.7
	2001	25.9	-2.6	-23.3	-4.4	-7.6	18.1
	2002	13.4	1.9	-11.5	-10.9	-10.5	17.5
	2003	4.4	22.0	17.6	8.8	16.2	16.8
	2004	9.6	23.3	13.7	9.0	10.7	13.6
	2005	10.9	22.8	11.9	9.2	8.5	8.7
Iceland – 50% Devaluation against all currencies 2007/2009	2005	4.0	7.2	3.2	7.5	4.6	2.6
	2006	6.7	9.8	3.1	4.3	8.4	2.9
	2007	5.1	8.6	3.5	5.6	5.2	2.3
	2008	12.7	8.3	-4.4	1.3	7.0	3.0
	2009	12.0	3.6	-8.4	-6.3	-5.9	7.2
	2010	7.1	4.7	-2.4	-4.2		7.6
	2011	4.0					

Sources: Liesner, Thelma, *Economic Statistics 1900-1983*, London: *The Economist*, 1985. IMF, *International Financial Statistics Yearbooks*, *Eurostatistics* and British, Argentine and Icelandic official statistics and International Labour Organisation tables.

It is widely feared that devaluations generate big inflationary pressures which are hard to control and which may lead to prices running away. This, however, is also a false fear. As the table above shows, the world has had plenty of experience of major currency changes and with reasonably well-run economies there simply is no evidence from economic history that devaluation produces more inflation than, at most, a short term blip compared to what would have happened anyway. Again, we have had recent experience of this in the UK. When we came out of the ERM in 1992, the pound fell against all other currencies by about 19 per cent. There was then a widespread fear that inflation would take off, but nothing of the kind happened. In fact, inflation fell from 5.9 per cent in 1991 to 3.7 per cent in 1992 and to 1.6 per cent in 1993, before stabilising for the next few years at not far above two per cent. Nor is it surprising that this should have happened. While it is true that if the pound goes down, import prices will rise, there are many other factors which come into play which tend to moderate rather than increase inflation. Interest rates tend to be lower. The government can afford to reduce taxation. Production runs get longer, lowering costs. Orders switch to domestic producers, thus avoiding now more expensive imports.

Can manufacturers really benefit?

It is also feared that if the pound went down, British manufacturing industry would be in such bad shape that we would have nothing to sell to the rest of the world even if the prices charged were much lower than they are now. Again, we need to look at the statistics to see what actually happened in the past, to give us a guide to what is likely to occur in the future. Perhaps the most telling figures are to be found in recent ONS figures, showing what happened after the 2007/2008 devaluation. Between Q3/2009 and Q3/2011, the value of exports of semi- and finished manufactured goods rose by an astonishing 27 per cent—from £44.7bn to £56.7bn.[1] Unfortunately, our imports also rose over the same period by 27 per cent. This started from a considerably higher base figure, so our goods trade deficit widened, but this did not prevent the UK's exporters from rapidly increasing their sales abroad over this period. There is, however, always likely to be a period after a devaluation when the benefits to exports take longer to come through than the increase in the cost of imports. There is no policy without some downsides, however, and it is important to recognise that this drawback is likely to apply whenever a devaluation takes place.

In fact, the key requirement for a devaluation to work successfully is that the so-called medium-term elasticities of demand for exports and imports are of the right size and direction. Numerous studies have been done on what these elasticities are and all of them cluster round figures (+1 for exports and -1 for imports) which show that devaluations, if reasonably competently executed, must improve export performance, reduce imports, reduce unemployment, and increase the growth rate, although there will be a two or three year period of adjustment, particularly to export performance. Estimates published in 2010 in IMF Working Paper WP/10/180,[2] covering 113 countries and regions in the world, reviewed all the available research work and academic literature on these elasticities. For the 27 most developed countries the mean export elasticity was 1.28 and the median value 1.14. The mean and median import elasticities were 0.97 and 0.88. Those for the UK were actually above the average at 1.37 for exports and 1.68 for imports. There is no reason whatever, on the basis of these figures, for believing that a major devaluation by the UK would not dramatically improve most of our economic prospects within a year or two and the current account balance after two or three years.

A bad track record?

Finally, there is the argument that we have tried devaluation many times in the past and it has not worked. It is true that, since World War II, the UK devalued in 1949 and 1967, when there were fixed exchange rates, and that there have been fluctuations—some of them downwards—in the international value of the pound since it started floating in 1971. Unfortunately, it is also true that inflation has been higher in the UK, at least until recently, than in most of the countries with which we trade and therefore reductions in the value of sterling were unavoidable. In fact, the situation was always worse than this. The 1949 and 1967 devaluations thus only made up for ground which had already been lost and those since 1971 have all been too little and too late. The truth is that sterling has been overvalued as long as almost anyone now alive can remember, sometimes more and sometimes less but always far too high. The most telling statistic of all as to whether a country has an over-valued currency is what happens to its share of world trade and here the evidence for the UK is damning. In 1950 our share of world trade was 25 per cent.[3] By 1970 it had dropped to 6.5 per cent.[4] By 2000 it had fallen to 4.4 per cent and by 2010 it was 2.7 per cent.[5]

6

Conclusion

There is thus a great deal to be said in favour of a big shift in policy towards getting the exchange rate down, while we still have the room for manoeuvre to achieve this objective in reasonable order. There are, however, two more compelling arguments for seizing the initiative to get this done as soon as possible.

The first is that the alternative to moving in this direction is going to be dauntingly awful. The state of the British economy is bad enough at the moment, but it is very likely to get worse. Growth has already ground more or less completely to a halt, while our borrowing is still increasing fast. This is going to mean that, without a radical change in economic policy objectives, we are bound to suffer from years of deflation, negligible growth and mounting unemployment as whatever government we may have struggles with increasing difficulty to balance the books. Do we really want to suffer year after year of privation and austerity when none of it is really necessary?

The second consideration is that getting the exchange rate down is a matter on which, in the end, we will have no choice. If we continue to run up huge debts which we cannot pay back, sooner or later we will run out of creditworthiness. We will then have no lenders from whom we can borrow on manageable terms. There will then be a major currency crisis and the pound will crash. The reality, therefore, is that we do not in fact have a choice about whether the pound is going to be devalued. This is going to happen anyway, whether we like it or not, before very long. The choice we have is whether we get this done in an orderly manner while we still have time for this to be arranged, or whether we wait so long that we finish up with a disorderly rout. There is unfortunately all too real a danger that this second choice may be made and that our policy makers will fight to the bitter end to keep the currency much stronger than it needs to be for us to be able to pay our way in the world. This would simply repeat and accentuate the catastrophic policy errors which we have already made for much too long.

Nor would the result of the misjudgements involved in letting this happen be confined to our economic future. It is likely that there would be profound political implications as well. Unfortunately, the whole of the moderate right and the moderate left has been involved, not only in the UK but also across nearly all of the western world, in promoting and sustaining the exchange rate policies which have served us so badly over the last few decades. As a result, there are already increasingly ominous signs of support for the political centre leaching away across all western countries. No governing class can afford to make too many mistakes, but this is what we see happening to us. If

CONCLUSION

this trend continues and politicians offering moderate policies lose traction on a major scale with the electorate, there is a very significant danger that their place will be taken by a very different sort of politics, based on fear and resentment. Its characteristics will be xenophobia, racism, nationalism, protectionism and irrationality. The cost of the policy mistakes which our policy makers have made on the exchange rate have not only had huge economic costs. If they continue, they risk a massive erosion of our democratic cohesion and our liberal democracy.

The stakes are getting very high. We very urgently need a major reassessment as to where our current policies are taking us. We now need to look much harder than has recently been fashionable at radical alternative approaches to the conventional wisdom which has clearly failed and got us into our current depressing and disastrous predicament. There is an alternative range of policies which we could choose to adopt, which would make unnecessary all the austerity and failure with which we are currently threatened. Now is the time to pluck up the courage needed to adopt a strategy which will put our economy back on track for the growth, full employment and national well-being which will be well within our grasp if we can only muster the clarity of thought and determination needed to put this strategy into practice.

Notes

1: Britain's Disastrous Exchange Rate

1. Morgan, T., *Thinking the Unthinkable,* London: Tullett Prebon, 2011, p. 7.
2. The Chancellor of the Exchequer's Autumn Statement to Parliament, 29th November 2011.
3. *Financial Statistics July 2011,* London, Table 14.1B, p. 215.
4. *International Monetary Statistics*, Washington DC: IMF, 2011, p. 743.
5. http://www.imf.org/external/pubs/ft/weo/2011/01/weodata/index.aspx

2: Origins of the Error

1. *International Monetary Statistics*, Washington DC: IMF, 2000, p. 114.
2. *International Monetary Statistics*, p. 980.

3: A More Competitive Exchange Rate

1. Liesner, Thelma, 'Economic Statistics 1900-1983', Table UK.15, *The Economist*, London, 1985.
2. 'Economic Statistics 1900-1983', Table UK.2.
3. 'Economic Statistics 1900-1983', Table UK.9.
4. Quoted on page 15 in an article by Nicola Smith, Head of Economic and Social Affairs at the TUC in *Fabian Review*. London: The Fabian Society, 2011.

4: What Is To Be Done?

1. *International Financial Statistics,* Washington DC: IMF, 2000, pp.16 &17.

5: Doubts and Objections

1. ONS Statistical Bulletin *Balance of Payments – 3rd quarter 2011,* Table E, London: Office for National Statistics, 2011.

2. *A Method for Calculating Export Supply and Import Demand Elasticities*, Working Paper WP/10/180, Washington DC: IMF, 2010.

3. Schenk, Catherine, R., *Britain in the World Economy*, Oxford: Blackwell, 2005, p. 463.

4. *International Financial Statistics,* Washington DC: IMF, 2000, p. 128.

5. *International Financial Statistics 2011*, Washington DC: IMF, p. 67.